Here For a Moment

101 Songs and Poems about Life, Including
Activities, Distractions, Dreams, Experiences,
Groups, Objects, Travels

Books by Matt Kavan

Flopping on the Deck
The Forest That Knows
Thirsty Dreams
Here For a Moment
Here's To
The Morning Catch

Here For a Moment

101 Songs and Poems about Life, Including Activities, Distractions, Dreams, Experiences, Groups, Objects, Travels

Matt Kavan

Matt Kavan
2014

First Printing: 2014

ISBN: 978-1-312-36884-2

Matt Kavan
www.mattkavan.com

Book Cover Graphics: The painting was created by Paul Kavan.

Ordering Information:
Special discounts are available on quantity purchases by corporations, associations, educators, and others. For details, contact the publisher at the above listed address.

Dedication

To lessons learned
Escaping the burn
And dreams to be
Journeys to see

Contents

Introduction

The world and living in it can be a pretty strange place, full of unknowns and surprises, good and bad, seems to go slow or it's over before you know it. In between are all sorts of things, such as what we do for work or non-work activities, different dreams we go after, a wide range of experiences, meeting different types of people, learning about different types of objects or concepts, and all the travels in between.

Here For a Moment is an overview of some of these different areas, including 101 songs or poems and organized in seven sections.

The first being Activities, such as the different types of things one actually spends their time doing, at least versus watching.

The second is what usually prevents you from doing more of your activities, otherwise known as Distractions. While taking a break here and there is generally expected for anyone, many times these can have a way to end up being a little more than that, with years eventually adding up into this or that distraction, such as watching TV. Again, it's there and can have a unique purpose, but it's always there, it never stops, with it's main purpose of keeping you watching, which is fine and everything if that's what you want to do, but life is short enough as is, no need to just flush it for the sake of convenience.

After which is the third section, Dreams, both literal and symbolic, the horizons or peaks we're heading towards on whatever paths we're on. They're the places or ideas that cause us to overcome obstacles, keep on trucking, and what can feel like an infinity of persistence. They can be shared with others or kept to yourself. When going to sleep, dreams are just getting started, integrating your experiences with its own file management system and in a way providing a summary of the whole thing, helping you to more easily identify the next step. Or, they can called nightmares, showing some horrifying experience that you seemingly have no control over, but usually if having enough times, they also get repetitive and just like a game, you can recognize them for what they are and they simply go away. Either way, defined or not, one can't ignore them, and if you have the perspective that they're the ones running the show while sleeping, and if people are sleeping for a quarter or third of their life, it's adds up and probably shouldn't be discarded so easily, dreaming is a part of being alive.

From a combination of these are the fourth section, Experiences, sort of a lessons learned from what happened in your activities or what you observed.

Groups is the fifth section and includes experiences with people, both good and bad, usually good when all together in the same boat, maybe not so much when going in different directions. You have friends for a while, but you end up doing different things and you have new friends. They're not the same but they're the ones you're with in the present time or situation.

The sixth section is about objects, how they can have different meanings for different people, for some a crutch to help out, for others an anchor holding them back. With objects are technology, good or bad but as it's constantly evolving, similar to nature, it's hard to really be against it but at the same time leery of the hype as it rarely lasts. Tools to use for your activities, no more or less.

The seventh and final section is Travel, or all the times you're moving from one place to another and what you see or experience along the way. In reality, you don't have to physically move in order to travel as travel is really about experiencing anything new and you could say the common definition of travel is probably the easiest way to do it, you visit the place and just watch or absorb everything, often exhausting in itself depending how different it is.

In summary, life can be a complicated thing, we're constantly trying to know more but when seeking the unknown, big or small, once you're there it's defined and no longer new, the unknown has moved on to somewhere else, hence forever trying to catch what can never be caught, but realizing it and doing it anyway.

Activities

A New Plan

Scan the horizon, look at the stars
Make a new plan, from wherever you are
Gather supplies, for the upcoming trip
Maybe triple, distractions are sent
Share it with others, or meant for you alone
Find a new treasure, maybe a home
A day or a weekend, could be a lifetime
Adapting and changing, leaving some signs
For others to follow, or keep covered up
Needing a refuge, away from the left
To stop or go forward, maybe look back
Make another plan, fill up the sack
Day in and out, always the same
Planning the purpose, activities to claim
Sometimes working out, or mostly will fail
Especially the new, gone are the rails

A Root or a Leaf

Some people struggle
Some people coast
Some people live
Some build a moat

Chorus
All of these different people
Following a tree
A cave or a struggle
A root or a leaf

Some have excuses
Some will never quit
Some run as fast as they can
Some do nothing but sit

Chorus

Some are entitled
Some paid their dues
Some light a candle
Some string up a noose

Chorus

Balloons Floating High

Where the day begins, the same as the end
Through circles of fire, as fast as you can
Scarred, burned, scraped and weary
Another day done in a hurry
Slow down, take a break is suggested
See a bigger picture for a new directive
Been there done that, climbed in the vines
Fun for a while until hangover inclined
The waste that was made, steps you've delayed
Taking so long, to recover the stray
The expected result, discarded with glee
Balloons floating high, body to sea

Beyond the Bend

Where we go, what we do
End of the day, seeking true
The mountains to climb, bridges to cross
Rivers to find, in forests when lost
Sometimes a battle, maybe a chatter
Finding directions, in mazes of matter
Every day, waking up to do it again
Make it through, beyond the bend

Counting

Some people count
Others not so much
Maybe depending
On your crutch

Empty the Cycles

Empty the barrel
Empty the bottle
Empty the flask
Empty the fodder

Chorus
When all is empty
Fill it up again
These are the cycles
Tending to mend

Empty the tube
Empty the paper
Empty the web
Empty the clatter

Chorus

Empty the wants
Empty the choices
Empty convenience
Empty the voices

Chorus

House of Cards

It started so small, with just the three
Stacked with a roof, harmless to be
Add a few more, what could it hurt
A whole pack is gone, a Babylon spurt

Many more later, the years flying by
The house of cards, reaching the sky
All fine indeed, the builders declared
We'll sell it to all, a made up world

After a few years, it covered the place
Enclosed everything, nobody could escape
The days of old, now legends and myths
Long forgotten, in mirrors that twist

Diamonds are shiny, a carrot for choices
Hearts are lovely, for wants seeking voices
Clubs are blunt, a stick to behave
Spades are doors, call them a grave

Getting so high, the clouds give a sigh
How many times, the bubbles will rise
With a puff and blow, the house falls to dust
The tree feels the ground, connected with roots

Measure the Weight

Actions or words
Measure the weight
History is written
Future or fate

Momentum

Is momentum good or bad
Hard to say with tendencies had
Linger on or staying past its due
Feel the change and fanning the new

Even with just a little, hurdles are cleared
A snowflake announces, avalanche feared
No doubt, momentum has power
Even the lie begins to flower

Is it surface or deeper, could be the question
The wind or current, a river reflection
Or something more, beyond any measure
Trivial is time, seasons for weather

Just another tool, call it a springboard
Getting much faster, the ends are sewn inward
Neither good nor bad but a matter of signs
Dependent on steps, directions inclined

No More Plans

Plans within plans within plans
So many plots to hide the command
Fun and games to rule the day
Moving pieces for parts to play
Wants and choices the foundation to set
Kings to pawns the futures met
Where it ends nobody knows
Some say knives and bullet holes
Take until the last a cornered beast
After the storm a calming peace
Or so you'd think but haven't seen yet
Look at nature for a truer intent
Millions of species fighting to conquer
Driven to breeding themselves longer
With no ending or awareness
Bubble and bust going for ages
Some say a balance or interdependence
If looking longer maybe deliverance
Rising and falling a repetitive creation
Forms of clay in similar motions
Exciting as a clock hanging on the wall
Mostly the same but different from all
What to do different to change from the fate
No more plans from derivative stays
Keeping focus on the tasks of the day
Following dreams to light up the way

Receivers

We're all types of receivers
It's in our DNA
Only needed is the different
Sparking games to play

Sea or Stars

Chop down a tree
Burn up a bridge
What we do
Until another ledge

How far can you go
In the wind and rain
Can you be all alone
Without going insane

It might depend
On your given crutch
When to stand
Or creep and lurch

In the end
How to know where you are
An ongoing trend
The sea or stars

Sparkles and Stars

Some people count, so many things
Watching the clock, objects there is
All kinds of money, status aplenty
Rack up the score, seeking the honey
How many sparkles can you see in the waves
How many stars at the end of the day
Quite a few when playing the fool
No longer hiding, out of the noose

Who's In Command

Some people talk
Of nothing but plans
Others to act
Their own in command

Distractions

A Common Reaction

When all your attractions
Are blissful distractions
Forever you'll be
A common reaction

Answers of Change

The instant karma of pride
For the one who brags
Doesn't make it through
Answers of change

Baggage to Battles

Freeing the baggage
What can you do
Some say a battle
At least one or two
Gather your energy
Focus on the need
No longer trivial
The shoes on your feet

Bouncing Through

Bouncing through
The rings of fire
Feel the burn
Rising higher

Distractions Might Be

Not always so bad, distractions might be
Taking a break, take in the scene
Find a new course, from stuck in the mud
Maybe unwind, a game in the sun
But a slippery slope, distractions might be
Making a habit, losing some dreams
Choices are found, walk the trapeze
Wanting to fall, soaring the need

Expense Well Spent

Buy a ticket, take a ride
Killing time, don't ask why
In the end, start over again
Round and round, is the trend
Getting sick, too many spins
Off you go, getting thin
To the next, up and down
Might be over and underground
How long it lasts, getting tired
Need to sleep, get inspired
Getting rested, shed a skin
After awhile, wake again
What to do next, maybe different
No more rides, a kind of torment
No more money, hit the road
Where it goes, a need to know
So long, farewell, have a new game
Trying to stand but feeling lame
Too many crutches, far too long
Start by crawling, hear a song
Next thing you know, start to dance
Feel the beat, take a chance
Win or lose, you gain in the end
When your own, expense well spent

Grown From the Lair

Play all your games
I don't really care
It's all the same
Grown from the lair

Knowing the Worth

Some say there are beings
Surrounding the earth
I say good luck
Outer the worth

Loneliness

Some say it's lonely
When being alone
I prefer silence
A message from home

Messages

Seeing the messages
Falling everywhere
Some take everything
Others a fare

Weapons No More

Removing weapons, that sap energy
One at a time, together complete
Such a fine line, walk in the fog
Seeing the signs, the sun all along

When the tornado rises, find a place inside
When the dog is hungry, feed it with mind
When illusions surround, fall to the ground
When statues move in, Quixote is found

When knives are sharpened, see a picture trending
When traps are setting, silence for mending
When mirrors are shown, find a good stone
When all is known, become unknown

There's quite a few more, a repetitive bore
Find them in nature, a book or a store
All these weapons, single or together
Makes for a storm, always the weather

When all wiped away, born every day
Falling and rising, finding the way
Ride out the storm, land on the shore
Without your fuel, the weapons no more

Whatever You Want

Watch the TV
Watch the show
Whatever you want
No paddles to flow

18

Dreams

Always Loot

Sitting in the dried out grass
Thinking of all the adventures past
Seeing the new, greener shoots
From the dreams, always loot

Another Unknown

Are dragons real, where do they come from
No fossils found, but legends are tons
Each and every culture, has a few stories
A dinosaur remnant or hallucination
Connecting again in the modern trend
Spikes in the mind, messages send
Where or where, could they be seen
If listening to ancients, could be in dreams
Or nightmares you'd say, planting some seeds
Choices to follow, adding to scenes
Where you have a part, can rise or fall
Lessons to learn, bring back to it all
Maybe yes, maybe no, nobody seems to know
Are dragons real, another unknown

Awake in Dreams

See all the boxes stacked up, from the ground to the sky
The spheres roll around, too independent to bind
The lines stretching out, map the outer space
Dots at the ends, even clocks can't escape

Chorus
Sleeping in reality, awake in dreams
Find a new order, learning to see
Sixty four steps, nine levels up and down
Seven rings to hear, a dozen surround

All these ideas, of space and time
Twisting around, hiding the signs
Call it coincidence, a fate you've found
A dream in silence, the path you've sewn

Chorus

Some go straight ahead, only snakes on the trail
Others full of curves, riding on the rails
Some are so steep, you're afraid that you'll fall
Even when you do, the lotus will stall

Chorus

When all's going fine, be ready for attack
Master of disguise, lots of tricks pull you back
Nothing you can do, the same old scene
Repetitive clues, dragons in dreams

Chorus

Colors

With red to begin
Blue in the end
Purple to bridge
Gold in the sun
So many more
Scattered in between
Trapped in diamonds
Freed in dreams

Dream Unknown

When you treat the world, in wants and choices
You become yourself, a mirror with voices
A house of cards, with just a subtle breeze
Crash to the ground, a winter freeze
There's so much more, than what's outdoors
Stepping by the fire, sitting on the floor
Watching the logs, burning up with the time
Seeing the coals, you'll never go blind

Chorus
Nature on the outside, dreams are within
Follow as needed, the turns and bends
Onto another, how far does it go
There is no end, for the dream unknown

Up through the night, with dreams taking flight
No more distractions, blocking your sight
From black comes the light, a dot to begin
Opening up, a scene transcends
Follow it along, a lake on a mountain
Through a town, could be where you belong in
Maybe not, gone in a flash
From light to black, the dream is past

Chorus

Onto another, on a wide open field
Or up skyscrapers, nature won't yield
Watching the sky, from blue to red
So much more, when gone to bed
Waking up again, the sun shining new
Back to your world, the journey or noose
Collecting experiences, thoughts for the trough
Feelings to feed, when the going gets tough

Chorus

Dream Worlds

Living in a dream world
Not real, says a fact
What you see what you get
Staying on the surface track
Of the present or the past
Illusions making clear
What about the future
Hide or conquer fears
An unknown road
Nothing is yet written
Integrated together
Forward is planted
Sort of like the dreams
Running in your mind
Putting in the pieces
Pictures are aligned
Where they go, what they mean
Yours to figure out
All the roads to explore
Waking up with a shout

Dreaming Curves

I'm dreaming of a home
Where I've never been
Following the signs
The down and upwards trend

Sometimes I don't see
Too blind or in a fog
What's in front of me
Losing where I belong

Other times it hits you hard
A diamond to the head
Changing everything you know
Escape from the dead

Falling Dreams

The fall never stops, the brakes are all gone
Illusions come traps, faster you're thrown
Try moving forward, plots only thicken
Distractions gather, a lotus ascending

Will I ever slow down, enough to breathe
It seems I'm only, picking up speed
Maybe one day, land in a cloud of dreams
Until it rains, melting everything

Falling again, there is no bottom
How long it's been, there is no tomorrow
Only the moment, stretching to ends
The light and dark, blinking to begin

Seeing some shadows, whisking on by
Only a glimpse, no time to ask why
What comes next, never can tell
Since the trek, from the ledge and fell

Falling asleep, waking up again
Lying in a field, a meadow in the sun
Was it all a dream, am I back for real
Planted as a seed, with roots to feel

From Present Surroundings

Batten down the hatches, barricade the doors
The winds getting stronger, arriving is the storm
For years it's been building, gathering the weight
Feel the momentum, rising towards the fate
Some are building arks, others finding caves
Climb a higher ground, escape the surging waves
The lions meet their match, vultures don't yet see
The only ones remaining, swimming in the sea
Some have seen the signs, the dolphins and the whales
Awakened with a start, turtles rarely fail
From one to another, where to have free reign
The land is on fire, an ocean full of chains
Floating in the breeze, much lighter than the matter
Adapting to the scene, a crazy type of hatter
Some say a dream, from a primitive extension
Others a need, from present surroundings

Left and Right

Left for the thief
Taking all you can
Right for the dream
Joker in command

Lighting the Way

What are your dreams
The future to know
The paths that you walk
Directions to go
The hurdles to clear
The tunnels to run
The bridges to cross
Finding the sun
After the storm
Braving the rain
Riding a boat
Breaking a chain
So many more
Defining the day
Purpose for moments
Lighting the way

Nap Time

Taking a nap, resting for later
Getting recharged, an empty platter
Physical and mental, needing a break
Closing your eyes, for dreams to wake
Where they go, hard to remember
What do they mean, no letter or number
A story or scene, merging together
Times of the past, a future of feathers
Waking up again, all ready to go
Step on the stage, starting the show

Raining In Mind

With so many messages, all around everywhere
Some bad, some good, in the water, ground and air
You can ignore the lore, but you can never hide
Run as fast as you want, the battle's inside

In the sounds of silence, the messages flow
Can I receive, believe, directions to go
The fear is clear, breaking all the mirrors
Into the wild, nobody is nearer

Another day or test, convenience beyond the hedge
A challenge or quest, walking cross the bridge
A choice with a voice, singing from the sirens
With a word it grows, expanding from the island

Getting louder and stronger, can you feel the beat
Melting away, blocks of ice on your feet
Alive to survive, make it through another day
Discarding all lies, feel the truth to save

Starting so small, you can crawl over walls
Growing up tall, with roots you don't fall
Heading straight to the top, touching the sky
Circling around, it's raining in mind

Starting Inside

Some will try to smash your dreams
Chopping off every sprout
Maybe that's why they start inside
Where nobody is hanging out

Symbols

Why are messages sent in symbols
Too many directions for labels
With primitive words of meanings
Changing depending on leanings
Right or left, happy or sorrow
What works today, gone tomorrow
Call it a point, a star in the night
No matter the detour, remaining in sight
Some say a bird, a jay or a raven
Not a coincidence, karma is given
Staying silent, watching and listening
All of the signs, nobody is sending

Under the Radar

Walking the shadows, under a hood
Too many times, misunderstood
Symbols and signs, what do they mean
Night and day, myths and dreams
Best not to worry too much
In your mind illusions to clutch
Move through the edges, there and you're gone
No longer the hedges, to tell right from wrong
Careful with names, no need to announce
Unless playing games, purpose to count
Run into cats, crossing the path
Some are Siamese, others are black
When it gets to high noon, at the seaside saloon
Joined by the ravens, singing a tune

Experiences

Dry or Wet

The TV is static
Down goes the net
The storm has arrived
Are you dry or wet

Flowing in Blues

Seeing the cycles
Connecting the clues
Watching the signs
Flowing in blues

Getting Focus

The first step of avoiding a trap
Is knowing that it's there
So said a character
In a land left laid to bare

Learning the lesson
Another did decree
Escape repetition
Hell for you and me

Find the new to be alive
Is it wise or a fool
Is it out or inside
To be blind or seeing through

Going So Fast

With war on the news, a trough for the taking
Who will you choose, the fire or raining
From ground to sky and returning again
Trees to climb, on the boat a friend
Going so fast, what happened to it all
Atoms to smash, answering a call
The raven grabs the box, while nobody is looking
The joker has a laugh, the stars always watching

Inflation Blues

All these prices go up, I can no longer afford
Have to work harder every day
A downward spiral, it feels I've been hurled
In a world so full of chains

How to break free, is it a dream
Can I do it with a beer
A temporary escape, a relaxing way
To forget about all my fears

Of not quite making it, getting the call
Of a due I cannot pay
What comes next, a certain track
Nothing more I can say

Why can't we all work a few hours
Learning the rest of our life
Instead of giving so much, to so very few
Leaving the world with a crutch

I don't blame anyone, just following nature
The blind in a modern wasteland
The tragic course, we're all inclined
The waves will capture, our grains of sand

Laughing at the Signs

Looking into the eyes
Of the one that sees
Through all of the lies
Over centuries
What you'll find
Not a flinch or a blink
Just a steady gaze
Hearing you think

Say anything you want
Describe your woes and fears
Feel free to recant
Mistakes of the years
When you're finally done
Awaiting an answer
A giggle or a smirk
Responding with laughter

Not of your name
Not of your dues
Not of your pain
Not of your blues
Just of your questions
Welcome to earth
So many directions
What is the worth

The past is where you've been
The future is unknown
The now starts a trend
Reaping from the sew
What more there is
Changes all the time
Ignoring surface bliss
Laughing at the signs

No More Questions

I gave up on asking questions
A long time ago
Too much trouble
In the wind that blows

Power

Power can be so many, different types of things
Power can be loud, when nothing to sing
Power can be silent, holding back the blows
Power can be bought, when nothing to grow

Chorus
Some people say, it's where everything leads
Where does it start, maybe in me
Power for thoughts, the dreams in my mind
Power to feel, the path and the signs

Power can be a rumor, a story that's sold
Power can be a river, a place to go
Power can be addictive, always wanting more
Power can be saved, stored for the storm

Chorus

Power can be fast, lots of shiny objects and bells
Power can be still, in a world full of hell
Power can be healing, letting go the past
Power can be seeing, a future, free at last

Chorus

Questions and Perspectives

Questions
Don't believe the hype
Perspectives
Left when taking flight

Revenge

Getting revenge
Is always condemned
How does it help
The messages send
Righting the left
Order from chaos
Outside to balance
Struggles inside us
Maybe today
Maybe tomorrow
Maybe forgot
Lost is sorrow
But if not
It stews like a brew
Getting stronger
A harvest moon

Running

You always run faster
When being chased
So said the winner
Of another race

The Edges You Feel

When nothing works out
Welcome to the real
Only the broken counts
The edges you feel

The Troll

Collect your fee
A toll to see
Act the troll
Forever will be

Thieves and Jokers

A thief will steal
For objects to feel
A joker will know
The lines to sew
In the end, which is better
Never defined, by letter or number

Too Many Tickets

See the ones making rules
Writing all their tickets
In the end hearing only
Screaming and crickets

World of Power

In a world of power, where does it go
Getting so loud, the story is sold
For a clock or an object, it's all the same
At the end of the day, melt in the rain

In a world of power, where does it go
Might makes right, nature does know
With all types of peacocks, prancing around the fire
All the choices and wants, make the flame go higher

In a word of power, where does it go
Taking everything, no more seeds to grow
Synthetic replication, a machine is born
No longer alive, no uniqueness shown

In a world of power, where does it go
The minds are falling, into a black hole
Call it the end of the day, the death of a dream
The only power left, flowing down the stream

Groups

Boat Friends

Riding a boat
Which one are you in
If it's the same
Finding are friends

Changing Worlds

Some flocks are helpful
When new to the game
A type of refuge
Safe for the stray
But give it some time
And stake your own claim
The world that you see
Forever has changed

Circling Cages

The freer you are
The more they'll try to cage you
So said a bird
Waking up in the zoo

Enjoying the Moment

Some people say, life's full of choices
Never bother to listen, to the screaming voices
Others will tell you, that life's full of wants
Never enough, since learning to count

Chorus
You can say this or that, I really don't care
Have seen quite enough, beyond compare
I'd just like to sit here, relax from the torment
Feeling the sun, enjoying the moment

Some people say, life's all convenience
Never trying to struggle, for independence
Others will tell you, friends through it all
Rarely in the hardest, times that we fall

Chorus

Some people say, you gotta work much harder
Never started at the bottom, an empty platter
Others will tell you, it's all who you know
Never been different, on the stage of the show

Chorus

Envy and Wrath

Envy and wrath
Such a tragic path
Always the end
Barren to catch

Fame

What is fame
A position to claim
Cash in a name
An ace in the game
Until it gets lame
Stuck in the same
A picture to frame
Nobody to blame

Friends For a Tune

We're all alone
Ain't it the truth
Hop on a boat
Friends for a tune

Groups

Groups are defined
By purpose inclined
Preferring comply
Or else deny
If you decide
You can join the ride
Be on a side
Make a few signs
But if you try
Start asking why
Have something to hide
Thinking to fly
It's probably best
To keep it inside

Isolation

What is isolation
Alone with yourself
The fallen call it heaven
Others a kind of hell

Part of a Scene

Some people say
They're part of a scene
Mostly a drag
Pride to deceive

Relationships

Some are temporary
Shipmates in a storm
Best of friends, tired and weary
To the bay, is the norm

Sands of Dunes

Meeting friends of the past
Like an old forgotten tune
Taking a while to get back
Rowing in sands of dunes

Setting the Stage

I don't want your forgiveness or your pity tonight
I'll keep my errors, won't forget the sight
Lessons to carry, tricks in my bag
Never repeat again, I should be who says thanks

For teaching to be wary, of someone like you
Only the surface, never embrace the fool
Serious as a shark, the humor of a clock
Never lost a thing or escaped the flock

It is I who feels sorry, but there's nothing I can do
To share a perspective, something you have to go through
A pig in the wilderness, a sheep for the sheer
Security provides, never alive with fear

Just a little bit, to keep you on your edge
Real life consequences, wake from the dead
Learning how to die, thousands of times
For each and every one, learning to rise

Maybe that's why, all my lines seem out of line
Not many straight, falling down are signs
All tragedy, setting up the stage
For comedy, to settle the day

The New Weird

I am weird
So are you
If not we'd all be
Nothing new

Objects

Cellphone Sacrifice

Everyone on cellphones
The modern way to go
Only the here and now
Are sacrificed to know

Everyone Knows Everything

What happens when everyone knows everything
Is there nothing left to sell
All the adventures and experiences documented
All the rings of the bells

What happens when everyone knows everything
Are there no taxes to collect
All revenue and currencies burned
The fuel from an ancient

What happens when everyone knows everything
What to do day through night
All the equations are figured out
The different are silent

What happens when everyone knows everything
When we go to bed
The dreams that come from somewhere else
Streams of visions in our head

What happens when everyone knows everything
A pebble hits the water
Going on through the end of time
Rippling through the matter

What happens when everyone knows everything
And finding nothing at all
Know that too, and born you'll be
Crawling up the wall

Eyes

Looking past the surface
Of anything you see
You probably should be blind
For the eyes do deceive

Foolish Objects

Give me a stick, to carry a sack
Shoes with some holes, bells on a cap
Anything more, will leave on the floor
So says the fool, walking through doors
Or so it seemed, windows in dreams
Even the dog, knows what it means
Falling down fast, but no baggage for weight
Out of the sack, a carpet for flight

Frames

What is a frame
But the edge of a picture
Caging the strange
Within a receiver

Glasses

What is a glass
But something to fill
Or empty real fast
Seeking the thrill

How Many Apps

How many apps
How many choices
Can you adapt
Without the noises

Mirrors

So many mirrors, everywhere you look
Ancient was a lake, a pool in a brook
Maybe a shiny metal, reflective piece of glass
Along comes a photo, capture the past

Chorus
What's the harm, foul or token
Protection, reflections and reviews
Closing doors instead of open
Perspectives with infinite blues

Growing and spreading, a brand new house of cards
The web and video, through the home and yard
Driving in your car, speed traps and red lights
Drink in a bar, not just toilets for sights

Chorus

Past the Surface

See past the surface
If you think it's worth it
Don't be surprised
When the dream has died

Signs

See the new sign
An ad or a warning
To fall or to climb
Stopping or soaring

Status and Fame

Status and fame
Defined is the game
For others to claim
A present in chains
Call it insane
Needing the rain
Make again plain
Fermenting the grain

The Same Old New

Living in a box
Plugged into a tube
Which is more real
The same or the new

Hard to tell it seems
Unlimited choices on call
What about when you fail
How far do you fall

Or how about the dreams
Where do they go
The unknown worlds
Glimpses to show

It seems that the trend
Of reality in truth
Around the next bend
Steps to the new

Types of Objects

Some are functional, tools of the trade
Some are traditional, collections made
Some are symbols, of derivative meanings
Some are valued, dependent on timing
So many objects, with all types of reasons
Perspectives or hollow, alone or a system
All the same, when beginning to rain
Washing and growing, out of the brain

Zero

Starting from nowhere, zero knows the game
No need to define in a primitive way
No chickens are found, cliffs all around
Circles of snakes, have scattered the ground
Such a simple form, with nothing to hide
Only the seed, planted in mind
Where it goes, a surge or a fall
Sitting at rest to infinite calls

Travels

Border Crossing

Crossing a border
Not always so much fun
Mostly you'll get hassles
Rarely said and done
The ones with the power
Can do what they want
Ask a thousand questions
Judging day and night

Bus Ride

Riding on the bus
A boat for the moment
Until the next stop
All is in silence

Connecting Moments

When feeling stuck and not sure what to do
Hitting the road for escaping blues
See the world from others perspectives
Makes you think, internal reflections
Of what you thought hard, maybe not so much
Or taken for granted, not a random lunch
Either way, you'll see a bit different
Lighting up dots, connecting moments

Doors to Explore

On the lakes of Minnesota, drinking beer in Wisconsin
Falling down dunes in Michigan, in Illinois caught for speeding
Ohio was a show, Pennsylvania had a meeting
Boston beer and chowder, New York a foreign greeting
Catch the sun in Florida, take a walk in New Orleans
Caught in a storm in Texas, Puerto Rico was a scene
Ran into a ditch in Iowa, had some shots in Kentucky
Walked a street in Memphis, followed down the Mississippi

Chorus
All of these places and so many more
Each are unique, doors to explore
The smells and sounds, the vibe that you feel
Merging together, when settled in dreams

LA was a flash, stayed awhile in San Francisco
Nevada racing fast, Montana fire and snow
North Dakota slowing down, Canada for a rest
Caught a salmon in Alaska, finding Ireland a past
Ride a boat to Scotland, England hear a tune
Ride a bike in the Netherlands, Belgium beers at noon
In Germany have some more, resting cheers in Krakow
Questions rise in Prague, in France the time to slow

Chorus

Parties in Barcelona, through the ancients of Italy
Greece with islands and warmth, to music on roofs in Turkey
Walk the sands in Egypt, see the lions and crocs of Kenya
The peaks and towns in Nepal, steam baths in Rotorua
Dumpling dishes in Hong Kong, a Tsingtao in Shenzhen
Some Saki in Japan, in Seoul was music till the end
Spicy dishes in Taiwan, some tunes in the Philippines
Hawaiian waves are crashing, in Mexico rice and beans

Chorus

Driver Finding Thrills

A road trip in the mountains
Curvy roads and hills
Hang on for your life
For the driver finding thrills

Ends and Means

The ends justify the means
Causing the journey quickly to cease
The moments are gone, what has been found
A foundation of steps, all going down

What are means but tendencies
Gathering together from infinity
Being defined by actions inclined
Or letting go and seeing the signs

That take you farther than plans can dream
An unknown thought planted to seed
Forgetting the past, anchors to cast
What it means, moments to last

Getting Out

Getting out and seeking perspectives
Towards a city or nature inspections
Maybe for work, a family vacation
On a weekend or afternoon distraction
See what others are doing or sharing
New ideas, discovered creations
Returning again, refreshed or inspired
Reset a plan, logs in the fire

Here For a Moment

Starting the day, who knows where it leads
Follow a plan or detours to be
Highs and lows, getting things done
By late afternoon, time in the sun

To take a nap, soak up the rays
Finding a break when nobody says
Before the evening and festivities ahead
Make a new plan or head off to bed

Or meeting a person, have a conversation
Sharing perspectives, a contemplation
So rarely the same, the paths that we go
Here for a moment, all that we know

Lighthouse Illusions

Across the stormy seas a lighthouse is decreed
Refuge from the weather of life that's made to bleed
Getting closer to the anticipated bay of reflection
Rocks and waves break up the hope and intention
Circling around to try another tack
The same as before but stabbed in the back
To move on or try again the question is raised
After another, call it a hundred, no longer debate
Looking back one last time it's not the same as before
The moon it seems, a mirage or dream, maybe too long from the shore
Back to the sea, a fate will be I'll leave the rest on ignore
Illusions will bring for wants that sing leaving you scarred and gored

Lines

Follow lines
Through rings of signs
Past or future
Gone is time

No Matter the Change

Right over left
No matter the change
A joke or theft
Familiar or strange

Sitting and Waiting

Sitting and waiting
Ready to spring
Staying prepared
What fate will bring

Sticking With Shoes

If you ever see a dragon
Sitting and relaxing
Give it all your coins
Using as a taxi

Across the lake
Or up to the stars
A command to take
Out of the yard

Anything else
Will be happy to please
Until you are out
Of energy

Discarded at will
Chucked in the fire
Letting it loose
All your desires

Thinking it through
Where over how to go
Sticking with shoes
All that's needed to know

Stuck on the Ground

Feeling lost
A stranger in the town
No matter where you go
Still on the ground

Trip 76

Hearing the messenger, in the sounds of silence
See the rising sun, breaking the horizon
Walking through a passage, another perspective
Putting on your armor, a Quixote directive

Sitting on a bench, looking for what's missing
Along comes a bird, singing and chirping
A fog rolling in, can't see what's ahead
Need to find a boat, escaping the dread

Find a hole in the wall, see the light again
Walk across the bridge, thinking that I can
Getting faster and stronger, bullish to the end
Afterwards who knows, starting over a trend

Reaching a new balance, healing to go forward
Laying a foundation, with steeples on the corners
Watching for the shadows, six senses are becoming
Melting all the chains, from the mind in dreaming

Staying in the new, the child and the fool
Connecting in a circle, making it through
The clouds start to gather, a message for you to hear
Over the dog that barks, when getting too near

A hope for a rise, with roots planted in the ground
Follow along the signs, visions that are sound
Creations from your ashes, a test you'll try to pass
Order from the chaos, the fish are swimming fast

Announcement of the dawn, after a very long night
The flowers start to open, receive the morning light
Circling the globe, from a fresh new idea
The grapes overflow, a glass and a cheer

Building up your courage, hammer home the point
Giving and receiving, with hands to anoint
Open up your heart, energy is flowing
Down to the ground, hoeing for aplenty

Hear the horns and trumpets, time for the charge
Breaking from the gates, horses in the yard
Leaving from your home, protected for awhile
Back to the ice, contemplate denial

Finding the secret key, open all the doors
Walking with a light, a lantern showing more
Through a figure eight, stretching with no end
Falling with a bolt, the lightning quick to send

Landing on a lily, growing from a tear
Maybe try a lion, saving over fear
Strolling in the sun, a lizard shows the way
To the rocky shores, a shell of former days

When the evening settles, awareness from the moon
Shining on the mountain, a quest embarking soon
Hear the screaming ocean, hints of a scene
Starting with a step, on paths of our dreams

Walk the middle ground, for pillars raising high
Only with your pitcher, waters won't deny
Pouring on your fields, reaping what you sew
Taste from the richness, the pomegranate to show

Make your own decision, with family and your friends
Misting in the morning, feel the raining cleanse
Heading out the door, determined as a ram
Breaking from the knots, of ropes that tie our hands

Through a field of roses, every hope has a price
Putting in your dues, no need to measure twice
Discovering a scroll, glimpses from the ancients
Covered by a shield, hiding all the moments

Of ideas and perspectives, ships for new directions
Travel with a snail, a home is where your heart is
Shedding all your skins, adapting to the weather
After falling snow, crystallize the matter

Answering the riddle, open up the gates
Picking up the staff, purpose to awake
Clearing up your vision, through glass of different shades
Gazing at the star, direction never fades

The sun has it all, every part of the journey
Sides that will show, flowers and their leaning
Rising from the tomb, with a new understanding
A trinity is found, for balance and creating

Reassess some walls, open or protection
When the water falls, eliminate distraction
Howl at the moon, finding your own path
Laying down the wreath, standing to the last